íRísh bíRos

by Paul Hillis

Irelan[d]
eagles,
marsh
today [
tion an
century

INTRODUCTION

Welcome to Ireland where, it has been said, the impossible happens always and the inevitable never. A cuckoo has been known to lay in a black-headed gull's nest here.

The breeding birdlife of Ireland has a northern rather than southern flavour with several subarctic breeding birds such as red-throated diver, common scoter and black guillemot reaching their southern limit here, whilst no southern species achieves the reverse. Migrant birdlife, on Europe's western fringe, has strong oceanic and North American elements. Shearwaters from the South Atlantic are regular visitors and North American waders relatively frequent vagrants during autumn passage, whilst Ireland's wintering white-fronted, brent and barnacle geese all nest in Greenland or Arctic Canada.

Ireland's mountains and forests are modest, but there are unusually extensive lowland moors or boglands. The coasts are interesting, with good estuaries and some fine seabird islands and mainland cliffs, but the numerous lakes probably form Ireland's greatest asset. Some are extremely large, several areas have swarms of small lakes, and some mountain glens have deep narrow lakes. A number of turloughs – richly vegetated limestone lakes with underground drainage – survive, but many have now vanished under farm drainage schemes.

In describing some of our more interesting species, this book is intended as an appeal and an invitation to Irish people and visitors alike to enjoy and take pride in wild birds. Unfortunately many people still think that there is something childish about simply enjoying their presence.

Many species live successfully in man's world, but human activities lost

returned and has since spread vigorously, the marsh harrier may soon follow and several new species such as the collared dove and reed warbler have started to nest; in addition a programme of re-introduction of the white-tailed sea eagle is being undertaken. The mild winters benefit such species as the **KING-FISHER (cover)** and result in great increases in numbers of winter visitors when hard weather strikes the continent. With increased public interest and concern, this winged heritage has great potential for further enrichment in diversity and numbers.

1 Common buzzard

Like most west European countries, Ireland has a large proportion of farmland, with much more pasture than arable land. The land varies greatly in quality, being generally better in the east than the west.

Farms, as sources of grain or insect food with numerous hedge-nesting sites, attract many widespread and abundant bird species, and several scarcer ones have interesting distribution patterns. In certain areas near the sea or Lough Neagh, the ubiquitous house sparrow is joined by its less raucous relative, the **TREE SPARROW (2)**. This species, almost extinct here in the early fifties, has since made a vigorous comeback.

Swifts, swallows, martins, some warblers and other insect feeders are of course summer visitors, and one of the most attractive is the **WHINCHAT (3)**. The male's cheerful song may be heard from patches of whin and hedges in rough pastureland across the midlands from Wicklow to Sligo and in the north, but elsewhere it is surprisingly rare.

Of all the birds of the Irish countryside, none is a more familiar memory to the older generation than the **CORN-CRAKE (4)**. This voice of the bright May meadows of many parts of Ireland could be heard at all hours thirty years ago, but has now declined almost to vanishing point in many areas due to the destruction of mother and brood during silage cutting, which takes place much earlier than the traditional hay cutting which it has replaced. Only in some mostly remote areas where hay is still grown, such as the Shannon callows (water-meadows) and parts of the north and west does a small remnant survive.

The barn owl, that elusive white ghost that hunts over the fields by night, is sadly also in decline, due it is thought to a decline in suitable nest-sites and possibly food supply. However, reasonable numbers still find nesting places in the ruined abbeys and castles that abound in many parts of Ireland.

The crow family is much in evidence on farmland, and in Ireland the handsome grey and black **HOODED CROW (5)** replaces the all-black carrion crow of most of Britain and western Europe. Hooded crows commonly feed in the fields along with rooks, jackdaws and magpies, and nest on the edge of adjoining woods.

2 Tree sparrow

3 Whinchat

4 Corncrake

5 Hooded crow

WOODLAND BIRDS

Woodlands are the ancestral home of most birds which have colonised our gardens, and indeed the most common species encountered there include such familiar garden birds as the chaffinch, robin and blue tit.

Two main types of woodland are the coniferous plantation, often of trees of the same age and species, and the more natural deciduous wood, now largely restricted to mountain valleys too steep for agriculture, and to some old estates.

Coniferous woodland can be rather monotonous as the trees rise vertically in dark closely planted ranks, but a few birds in addition to the adaptable species mentioned above can always be found there, notably the **COAL TIT** (**6**) and goldcrest. The siskin also nests in coniferous woods but moves out in winter to gardens or to riverside alders where it often joins feeding flocks of redpoll and goldfinch. An interesting development in recent years has been the increase in numbers of the erratic, roaming, gregarious crossbill turning up and sometimes nesting in our older coniferous woods.

Deciduous woods contain a greater variety of birds, garden birds again being the most numerous, along with the chiff-chaff, willow warbler and less common **BLACKCAP** (**7**), a garden visitor in winter. The rarer garden warbler prefers forests bordering large loughs such as Erne, Neagh and Ree, while three extreme rarities, the redstart, wood warbler and pied flycatcher, nest in some years in the glenside oak woods of Wicklow and elsewhere.

The larger woodland birds – the wood pigeon, jay, ground-nesting woodcock and two predators, the sparrowhawk and widespread but elusive **LONG-EARED OWL** (**8**) – inhabit most types of wood, though this owl has some preference for conifers.

6 Coal tit

7 Blackcap feeding young

8 Long-eared owl at ne

FRESHWATER BIRDS

Each of the different freshwater habitats has its own characteristic birds. The **DIPPER** (9) is at home surrounded by waterfalls and damp mossy rocks of swift, tumbling streams, the **KINGFISHER** (**cover**) requires the steep earth bank of a mature river in which to dig its nesting tunnel, and the **HERON** (10) likes shallow water for feeding with tall trees nearby for nesting.

The numerous lakes hold breeding mute swans, ducks, coots, moorhens and grebes, Lough Neagh having large numbers especially of tufted duck and **GREAT CRESTED GREBE** (11). The rarest European bird breeding on Irish lakes is the **COMMON SCOTER** (12) which breeds in small numbers on several large limestone lakes in the midlands, west and north-west. The rare and beautiful black-necked grebe used to nest on some western turloughs, but very seldom does so now due to the deterioration of its haunts.

9 *(below)* **Dipper with food**
10 *(bottom)* **Heron at nest**

In winter the large lakes carry great flocks of diving ducks. At its peak season Lough Neagh can have forty thousand, mainly pochard, tufted duck and goldeneye, and is unique in its large freshwater contingent of scaup. Lough Corrib supports up to twenty thousand, mainly pochard, and many lakes have the three more common species in winter, and also **COOT** and **MUTE** and **WHOOPER SWANS (inside front cover)**. **BEWICK'S SWANS (25)** are considerably more local, but tend to be more gregarious where they do occur.

Flooded turloughs, such as Rahasane, and callows along the Shannon, Little Brosna and Suck can hold wigeon, teal, plovers and sometimes black-tailed godwits in thousands, with fair numbers of shovelers, pintails, geese, swans and **COMMON SNIPE (flap)**. Such areas are now tending to disappear due to drainage schemes, however, and the survival of the great flocks depends on the conservation of some undrained wetland sanctuaries.

11 *(below)* **Pair of great crested grebes at nest**
12 *(bottom)* **Female common scoter with young**

BIRDS OF BOG
AND MOUNTAIN

As well as upland moors, Ireland has great irregular tracts of heathery bog interspersed with farmland in many low-lying areas. Three of the most attractive songbirds of the heather are the **STONECHAT (back cover)**, wheatear and ring ouzel. The wheatear is usually confined to rocky terrain while the stonechat also inhabits flat lowland bogs. The ring ouzel is now rare, surviving most numerously in areas of cliff and scree slopes.

The most specialised of the heather nesting birds is the **RED GROUSE (flap)**, which is widespread, though less abundant than on the carefully managed moors of northern Britain. Waders, such as snipe and curlew, also nest on bogs, mainly on the damper parts. Two birds of prey often nesting in the heather are the

HEN HARRIER (female with young, **13**) and merlin. The lively, aggressive harrier, almost extinct fifty years ago, made a healthy recovery, though it has declined again in most areas. It often breeds in young forestry plantations, where growing conifers make the area impenetrable to intruders without obliterating the ground space. By contrast, the small, swift merlin sometimes nests in trees, using old hooded crows' nests.

Upon the mountain cliffs the **RAVEN** (**14**) is currently extending its range, and slowly colonising trees and ruined buildings in the process. Its traditional neighbour the **PEREGRINE** (**15**), hard hit in the past by pesticide residues in its prey, now appears to be recovering well despite the theft of eggs or young from the nest, which sometimes happens.

14 Raven with young at

13 Female hen harrier with young at nest

15 Peregrine

Birds confined to wild and remote surroundings acquire a special charm of their own, and Ireland has several species which, although they are strictly mountain- or water-birds, seem to merit a section to themselves. Some of these are northerly birds at the southernmost extremity of their breeding ranges in Ireland.

A handful of pairs of **RED-THROATED DIVERS (16)** have bred for over a century by several small lakes in Donegal despite fluctuations in water level and human disturbance from time to time. These beautiful but timorous birds deserve every consideration from anyone lucky enough to discover their breeding haunts.

By contrast, the **COMMON GULL (back cover)** is a widespread breeder on lakes in Donegal and Connacht, with a scattering of small coastal colonies south to Kerry and east to Down. Breeding in small numbers on bogs in the north-west are the dunlin and golden plover, the latter generally being confined to high mountain areas.

Two birds which have, respectively,

colonised and recolonised the north coast from the west of Scotland are the **EIDER DUCK (17)** and **COMMON BUZZARD (1)**. On the cliffs of the north Antrim coast both may be seen together, rafts of eiders floating offshore whilst several buzzards soar aloft. The eider, which arrived in 1912, nests on most coasts between Sligo and Down, and the buzzard, absent as a regular breeder from 1890 till 1940, appears now to have a population of over a hundred pairs nesting in six or seven northern counties.

The red-necked phalarope abandoned its traditional Mayo colony from 1972 to 1978 since when it has made a rather faltering comeback, with one pair nesting in some years. The greenshank and dotterel have nested sporadically in recent years and the superb-looking goosander is slowly trying to colonise Donegal, a female with young on the water having been seen in several recent years. It also appears that the frequency with which Scottish golden eagles stray across to Ulster may be on the increase.

16 *(below)* **Red-throated diver on nest**
17 *(bottom)* **Eider duck on nest**

SHORE AND ESTUARY

In summer, many of the low-lying islands off the Irish coast hold colonies of terns or black-headed gulls. Common, Arctic and Sandwich terns breed on most coasts, but the rare and beautiful **ROSEATE TERN (18)** is confined to the east, where the majority of the seriously depleted west European population now breeds under strict protection on one island, with remains of formerly strong colonies on several others.

Many of the great mixed terneries, where a blizzard of birds used to greet visitors and the presence of eggs or young everywhere called for careful walking, have seriously decreased. Strong colonies on the Copelands and Burial Island (Down) have disappeared in the face of herring gull expansion and it is hoped that the recent fall in herring gull numbers will allow the terns to increase once more.

In winter, small parties of **SNOW BUNTING (flap)**, distinctive in white and sandy plumage, often visit the shore above the high tide mark, and around the ports the resident gulls may be joined by visitors. The glaucous gull winters

18 *(right)* **Roseate tern**
19 *(below)* **Ring-billed gull**
20 *(below right)* **Dunlin in summer plumage**

regularly in small numbers, especially at Killybegs and Galway, but may appear almost anywhere on the coast, as may the rarer Iceland gull. The little gull, however, visits the east and south coasts most frequently, usually during easterly winds. A newcomer, first seen in Ireland in 1979, is the American **RING-BILLED GULL (19)**, of which several dozen are now present in winter with a few remaining over summer; however, no Irish nest has yet been found.

The main change wrought by autumn is the invasion of tidal mudflats by wildfowl and waders, some of which pass on elsewhere, whilst others remain to winter. The greatest concentrations of waders, normally numbering over forty thousand, occur on Strangford Lough, Cork Harbour and Dundalk Bay, while the Shannon Estuary, Dublin Bay and Tralee Bay usually hold over twenty thousand. Lough Foyle and Strangford hold the most wildfowl, about twenty-five thousand each, while Wexford Slobs and Harbour have approaching twenty thousand.

The main waders are **DUNLIN** (in summer plumage, **20**), knot, **OYSTER-CATCHER** (on nest, **21**), curlew,

21 Oystercatcher on nest

22 Black-tailed godwit in summer plumage

BLACK-TAILED GODWIT (22), BAR-TAILED GODWIT and **RED-SHANK (23)**, with lapwing and golden plover if there are suitable fields nearby. Brent are the characteristic geese of the mudflats, and wigeon are often numerous, with **TEAL (24)** and some pintail, shoveler, mallard and shelduck. Dabbling ducks, grey geese and certain waders which also frequent fresh water often occur at combined estuary and fresh-water sites in greater variety and numbers than at purely tidal or inland haunts. Each estuary has its own speciality,

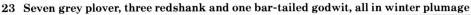

23 Seven grey plover, three redshank and one bar-tailed godwit, all in winter plumage

whether it be massive migration of black-tailed godwit on the Shannon in spring or golden plover wintering at Tralee. Bewick's and whooper swans flock together at Lough Foyle and numbers of **COMMON SNIPE (flap)** join the shore waders at Ballymacoda.

The mudflats of Wexford Harbour separate the North and South Slobs, reclaimed land protected by dykes, where ten thousand Greenland **WHITE-FRONTED GEESE (25)** winter, the bulk of that species' population in Ireland, often joining several hundred **BEWICK'S SWANS (25)** to feed on waste potatoes. A very few pink-footed and Canada geese also winter, and grey-lag, barnacle and blue snow geese appear some years, as well as partially white-headed birds which may be **WHITE-FRONTED × CANADA HYBRIDS** (one foreground, **25**). The Canada geese include birds of small races which migrate from northern Canada, as well as some of the large race acclimatised in Europe which are possibly strays from England but more probably genuine Canadian migrants, as indicated by their

Male teal

25 White-fronted geese, a hybrid goose (front) and Bewick's swans

29 Two male and a female red-breasted merganser

arrival with the white-fronts. The many ducks include shelduck and scaup on the harbour, while ruff and spotted redshank are among the more interesting waders. This remarkable area also holds such attractive birds of prey as the hen harrier, merlin and short-eared owl, which hunt over the wintry slobs along with the kestrels.

Half an hour from Belfast by car, the mudflats in the Newtownards area of Strangford Lough hold the largest flock of **BRENT GEESE (26)** in Ireland, fourteen thousand strong at their November peak and currently increasing; by contrast the **WIGEON (27)** feeding with them appear to be decreasing. Knot, dunlin and lapwing are the most numerous waders, and small flocks of greylag geese frequent the islands in the lough and the River Quoile below Downpatrick.

As a place for viewing wildfowl and waders, the North Bull Island **(28)** off the Dublin suburb of Clontarf has few rivals. Here, beside the main road, unconcerned **BRENT GEESE (26)** feed close to pram-pushing mothers and shoppers waiting for the bus (routes 30, 31, 31A, 32 or 32A). Teal, wigeon, pintail and shoveler have also responded to the sanctuary of the suburbs by becoming unusually tame and may be seen at especially close quarters from the causeway road at flood tide. As well as the more numerous waders, hundreds of grey plover occur, early migrants in autumn and late ones in spring being resplendent in summer plumage (seven **GREY PLOVER**, three **REDSHANK** and one **BAR-TAILED GODWIT** in winter plumage, **23**).

Diving ducks, grebes and divers frequently winter on sheltered waters. South across Dublin Bay, the West Pier at Dun Laoghaire is a good vantage-point for seeing goldeneye, long-tailed duck, common scoter, **RED-BREASTED MERGANSER (29)**, great crested grebe and red-throated and great northern diver in small numbers, while Slavonian grebe and black-throated diver appear occasionally. Merganser, goldeneye, great crested grebe and the commoner divers are widespread elsewhere, but only a few places like Portnoo (Donegal) have enough long-tailed duck to form their distinctive noisy, restless flocks. Common scoter winter in flocks off long exposed beaches, where velvet scoter also occur occasionally, mainly off the east coast.

26 *(top left)* **Brent geese**
27 *(centre)* **Two male and a female wigeon**
28 *(left)* **Evening at the North Bull Island**

CLIFF AND ISLAND

From April to July, cliff seabird colonies probably form the biggest spectacle provided by Irish birds. The ceaseless activity of guillemots, razorbills and kittiwakes against dramatic, scenic background is supported by a cast of fulmars, shags, cormorants and the larger gulls. The hole nesters, **PUFFIN (30)**, Manx shearwater and storm petrel, are largely confined to islands, the puffin having a marked preference for precipitous places.

The south-western islands – Blaskets, Skelligs, Bull, Cow and Puffin Island – hold the most impressive mixed colonies, Inishtearaght having Ireland's largest puffinery and possibly the world's largest storm petrel colony. The Little Skellig has Europe's second largest gannetry (**31**) with about twenty thousand pairs, and Puffin Island has Ireland's largest colony of Manx shearwaters. Mayo has substantial auk colonies on its islands and mainland cliffs, but their actual strength is not known. In Donegal, Horn Head has the largest colony of razorbills in Ireland or Britain, and a small mainland puffinery, while Doonmore Stack (**32**) and the adjacent cliffs at the west end of Rathlin Island (Antrim) have Ireland's largest guillemot colony. The Great Saltee (Wexford) has gannets and auks easily viewed on the low, though still dangerous, cliffs. Further colonies exist on other coasts.

30 *(below)* **Puffin with fish for young**
31 *(bottom)* **The Little Skellig gannet colony**

Numbers of puffins seem to have stabilised after a period of severe decline, which also affected guillemots and razorbills to some extent. The ever-increasing gannets, by contrast, have recently colonised Ireland's Eye off Howth, in the Dublin suburbs, and the mysterious Leach's petrel, last previously known to have bred here in 1906, was found to have a colony of about two hundred pairs on the Stags of Broadhaven off Mayo in 1982.

While seabirds are mostly restricted to a relatively few large colonies, most of the wilder cliffs have their **CHOUGHS (33)**. Ireland forms this species' headquarters north of the Alps, and the buoyant exuberant flight of flocks of fifty or more is still frequently witnessed in favoured precipitous areas. Some of these areas also harbour flocks of rock doves with the rare pure wild-type plumage, indicating absence of feral pigeon ancestry. With luck, people visiting the cliffs of west Kerry should have a chance of seeing at liberty the vanguard of the recently reintroduced white-tailed sea eagle.

The less exposed rocky coasts form Europe's southernmost breeding ground of the attractive little **BLACK GUILLEMOT (back cover)**. Ingenious nesting sites used by this species include holes in Bangor Pier and a wrecked ship near Portaferry (both Down) as well as inside the barrel of a cannon on the battlements of Carrickfergus Castle (Antrim).

32 *(below)* **Doonmore Stack guillemot colony, Rathlin Island**
33 *(bottom)* **Chough with young at nest**

The importance of strategically placed islands and headlands as landfall points for migrating birds, especially small ones, has long been known, but it was not until 1950 that Ireland's first bird observatory opened on the Great Saltee Island off County Wexford. The Copeland Bird Observatory (Down) followed in 1956 and Cape Clear, at Ireland's southern extremity in County Cork, in 1959. Sadly, the Saltee closed in 1964 and two Donegal observatories, Tory Island (1961–5) and Malin Head (1965–8), had even shorter careers. More recently, systematic observations have been made from Ramore Head (Antrim), the Mullet (Mayo), Bridges of Ross (Clare), Dursey Island, Old Head of Kinsale and Ballycotton (**34**) (all Cork), Hook Head (Wexford), Clogher Head (Louth) and St John's Point (Down).

In addition to finding that regular migrants like the redstart were more numerous than previously thought, the two south coast observatories found that a number of supposedly rare vagrants occurred annually, such as pied flycatcher, tree pipit, firecrest and even icterine and yellow-browed warblers. Irregular migrants recorded most years include **RED-BREASTED FLYCATCHER (35)**, melodious and barred warblers, red-backed shrike and ortolan bunting.

Cape Clear, though lacking the Saltee's huge numbers of common migrants such as the swallow, chaffinch and skylark, has enormous diversity in rarities, and since it opened has added twenty-four new bird species to the Irish list (twenty small landbirds including ten North American species, and four seabirds), compared with seven small landbirds (all European) added by Saltee between 1950 and 1964.

Northerly coasts have been quieter, but the Donegal observatories revealed regular passage of the Lapland bunting. Tory added five (European) birds to the Irish list during its lifetime, and Copeland has added two so far, oddly enough both American.

Migrating seabirds, many of which cover enormous distances, have also been watched systematically. Here again Cape Clear excels, with certain oceanic headlands also productive, such as Brandon Point, the Bridges of Ross and Ramore Head. Regular migrants include the skuas and the **GREAT SHEARWATER (36)** and sooty shearwater which both breed in the southern hemisphere and appear every year off the west and south-west in autumn, along with

34 Ballycotton wetland

35 *(top)* **Red-breasted flycatcher**
36 *(above)* **Great shearwater**

37 Pectoral sandpiper

Cory's shearwater, grey phalarope and Sabine's gull.

Wetland birds pausing on migration require suitable habitat, which is rare on the exposed islands, though Cape Clear has some. Lough Akeragh has a high volume of American waders, and added four new species to the Irish list. Other good haunts include Ballycotton, Cape Clear, nearby Lissagriffin, Tacumshin, the well-watched North Bull with four new Irish species, and Lough Beg north of Lough Neagh, the best inland location. The predominance of the south-west reflects an American contingent stronger among waders than songbirds. The **PECTORAL SANDPIPER (37)** occurs annually and the buff-breasted, Baird's and white-rumped sandpipers and lesser yellowlegs fairly frequently. American ducks visiting Ireland and often staying for the winter include the American wigeon, blue-winged teal and ring-necked duck, while the black and white-winged black terns are, respectively, regular and irregular autumn visitors from Europe.

One 'species' remaining all too scarce is the Irish ornithologist, although a number of 'migrants', mostly from Britain, contribute many worthwhile observations. We still know much too little about Irish bird-life and especially migration, and many vast gaps in our knowledge can only be filled by greatly increased numbers of reliable observers. Irish birds still offer mystery to intrigue and beauty to enchant many more enthusiasts than yet enjoy them.

ORNITHOLOGICAL SOCIETIES
British Trust for Ornithology has county representatives in Northern Ireland.
Cape Clear Bird Observatory Bookings Secretary, K. Grace, 84 Dorney Court, Shankill, Co. Dublin.
Copeland Bird Observatory Bookings Secretary, N. McKee, 67 Temple Rise, Templepatrick, BT39 0AG, Co. Antrim.
Irish Wildbird Conservancy Ruttledge House, 8 Longford Place, Monkstown, Co. Dublin.
Northern Ireland Ornithologists' Club Secretary, T. Lee, 7 Richdale Drive, Marine, Holywood, Co. Down.
Royal Society for the Protection of Birds Belvoir Park Forest, Belfast BT8 4QT.

ORNITHOLOGICAL GOVERNMENT AGENCIES
Department of the Environment Countryside and Wildlife Branch, Calvert House, 23 Castle Place, Belfast BT1 1FY.
National Parks and Wildlife Service Office of Public Works, 51 St Stephen's Green, Dublin 2.

Acknowledgements
Gerald Bond, front flap (bottom); C. Douglas Deane, 10, 11, 17, 32; Paul Hillis, 12, 24, 26, 28, 31, back cover (middle); John Ironside, 25; the late Tom Keogh, 3, 13, 14; Anthony McGeechan, 36; Richard T. Mills, front flap (top, middle), inside front cover, 2, 4, 6, 9, 15, 18, 19, 23, 30, 34, 35, 37, back cover (top); Kenneth Perry, 21, back cover (bottom); Ronald Thompson, 33; the late Lance Turtle, 20, 22, 27, 29. Wildfowl counts are quoted by kind permission of Ralph Sheppard, national counts organiser.